READING POWER

Working Together

Smoke Jumpers

Joanne Mattern

The Rosen Publishing Group's
PowerKids Press™
New York

Published in 2002 by The Rosen Publishing Group, Inc.
29 East 21st Street, New York, NY 10010

First Edition

Book Design: Erica Clendening

Photo Credits: Cover, pp. 4–19 © Mike McMillan/spotfireimages.com; pp. 20–21© Shmuel Thaler/IndexStock

Mattern, Joanne, 1963–
Smoke jumpers / by Joanne Mattern.
   p. cm. — (Working together)
Includes bibliographical references (p.   ).
ISBN 0-8239-5978-3 (lib. bdg.)
1. Smokejumpers—Juvenile literature. [1. Smokejumpers. 2. Wildfire
fighters. 3. Fire fighters.]   I. Title. II. Working together
(PowerKids Press)
SD421.23 .M37 2001
634.9'618—dc21
                                        2001000734

Manufactured in the United States of America

Contents

Smoke Jumpers

Smoke jumpers work as a team to fight forest fires that are burning out of control.

These firefighters jump from airplanes to reach the fires below.

Fireproof Suit

Smoke jumpers wear fireproof suits so that they won't get burned. They wear helmets, too.

At Work

Smoke jumpers land on the ground near the fire. They bring tools with them to help fight the fire.

Pulaski

The smoke jumpers cut branches from the trees. They drag the branches away.

Then they dig a ditch. This is called a fire line. The fire cannot spread because there is nothing that can burn.

Some members of the smoke jumping team fly helicopters. The helicopters can spray the fire with lots of water.

Staying in the Forest

Sometimes it takes a long time to fight a fire. That's when smoke jumpers stay in the forest. Smoke jumpers can rest in tents.

Smoke jumpers rest when the fire is under control.

They set up their camp. They sit together to eat.

Helicopters bring new supplies to smoke jumpers when they stay in the forest for a long time.

Smoke jumpers have a dangerous job. They depend on one another.

Smoke jumpers protect each other, too. Together, they work to save our beautiful forests.

Glossary

fire line (**fyr lyn**) an area where all burnable materials have been removed to stop a fire

fireproof (**fyr**-proof) almost impossible to burn

forest fires (**for**-ihst **fyrz**) fires that burn in wilderness areas

helicopters (**hehl**-uh-kahp-tuhrz) aircraft that fly without wings by using large blades that spin

Pulaski (puh-**las**-kee) a firefighting tool which can be used like an ax or hoe

smoke jumper (**smohk juhmp**-uhr) a firefighter who jumps out of an airplane to put out forest fires

tents (**tehnts**) movable shelters made of canvas or nylon that are held up by poles

Resources

Books

Smokejumper: Firefighter from the Sky
by Keith Elliot Greenberg
Blackbirch Marketing (1995)

Fire in Their Eyes
by Karen Magnuson Beil
Harcourt Brace & Company (1999)

Web Site

Hotshots
http://tlc.discovery.com/tlcpages/hotshots/
    hotshots.html

Index

Word Count: 199

Note to Librarians, Teachers, and Parents

If reading is a challenge, Reading Power is a solution! Reading Power is perfect for readers who want high-interest subject matter at an accessible reading level. These fact-filled, photo-illustrated books are designed for readers who want straightforward vocabulary, engaging topics, and a manageable reading experience. With clear picture/text correspondence, leveled Reading Power books put the reader in charge. Now readers have the power to get the information they want and the skills they need in a user friendly format.